The Spices of Morocco
The Most Aromatic Country in Africa

Geography Books for Kids Age 9-12

Children's Geography & Cultures Books

BABY PROFESSOR

EDUCATION KIDS

Speedy Publishing LLC

40 E. Main St. #1156

Newark, DE 19711

www.speedypublishing.com

Copyright 2017

In this book, we're going to tell you about the spices of the country of Morocco in North Africa. Let's get right to it!

Why Is Morocco A Hub For Spices?

Centuries ago, North Africa's coastal location was a central hub on the trade route for spices between Europe and the Far East. It was and is at a crossroads of several types of civilizations and cultures. Refugees came there from Iraq in the Middle Ages and brought with them their traditional recipes of fruit mixed with meat.

The Turks, Muslim refugees from Spain called the Moriscos, and the Berbers, who were the native people living in Morocco, contributed their best cuisine.

The result was one of the most flavorful and fascinating cuisines in the world–a combination that consists of European and Mediterranean, as well as the native Berber-Moorish cuisines.

Why Were Spices So Treasured In Ancient Times?

There was no refrigeration in ancient times, so food spoiled very quickly. The addition of spices helped to make food taste better and as a result spices were prized more highly than silver and gold.

The trade route where spices were carried from China to the Middle East to Africa and then to Europe was just as important as the Silk Road. For example, cinnamon was so sought

after in the first century AD that only 12 ounces of it could be purchased with 11 pounds of silver!

The Spice Souks Of Morocco

If you were visiting Morocco, you would soon come across the souks, which are open-front, marketplace stalls typically in the old quarters of the cities. Here, sellers display colorful and aromatic mounds of different spices in baskets. It's a feast for the eyes because of all the different colors and the smells are absolutely tantalizing!

The delicious cuisine of Morocco uses blends of spices from around the world. Cinnamon, paprika, saffron, coriander, white pepper, cloves, red chili, and sesame are used in blends to create flavorful stews, meat entrees, and desserts.

In addition to the colorful rainbow of spices offered, the markets are also full of just-picked fruits and vegetables, freshly caught fish, a huge variety of beans and lentils, grains of all types, and an abundance of different olive oils.

Ras El Hanout, The Traditional Moroccan Spice Mix

In addition to spices used to flavor foods on their own, there are many unique spice blends that are created for use in Moroccan cuisine.

One of the traditional mixes is called ras el hanout, which means "head of the shop." This name comes from the tradition of spice shop owners creating their own unique blends, sometimes with up to 100 different spices. As a result, ras el hanout became the common name for these mixtures.

Today, the typical ras el hanout generally has more than 20 different spices mixed together in varying quantities to make a rich, satisfying blend. Cardamom, anise, mace, ginger, cinnamon, various types of peppers, nutmeg, and turmeric are some of the spices frequently used in ras el hanout.

The taste of ras el hanout is something like curry. It has a floral, spicy aroma and its flavor is robust and yet subtle at the same time. This spice blend is frequently used on poultry or fish before grilling, baking, or

pan-frying. It gives the food a golden hue and a tasty, mild, sweet-smelling spiciness. It is used with lamb, dishes made with game, tagines, which are dishes cooked in special earthenware pots, and couscous.

Spices Used In Moroccan Cuisine

Many of the spices and other ingredients used in Moroccan dishes are cultivated and produced in the country. Saffron is cultivated in the city of Tiliounine, olives and mint come from Meknes, and lemons and oranges come from the city of Fez. Here are some of the most common spices used in Moroccan cooking, arranged from those that are used frequently to those that are used less often.

Kosher Or Coarse Salt

Coarse salt is used for cooking and table salt, which is finer, is used on food after the dish is prepared. All coarse salt varies in its level of "saltiness" so cooks have to be careful when they use it not to over salt the dish.

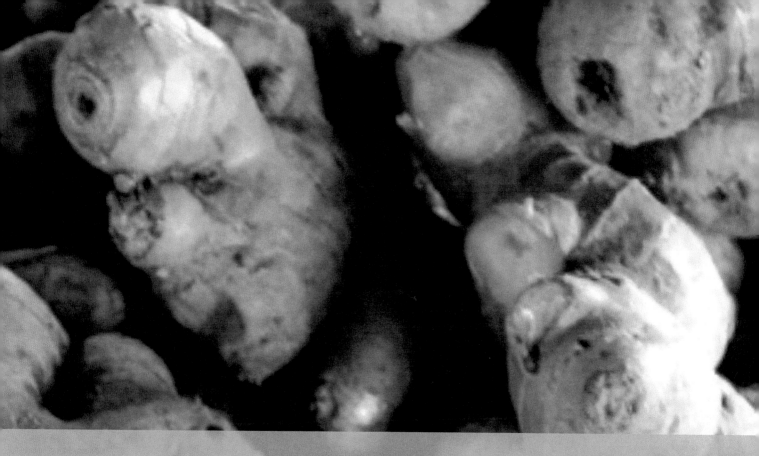

Ginger

Dried ginger comes from the ginger rhizome, which is an underground root. It is very spicy and fragrant. It's a common ingredient in the staples of Moroccan cooking such as soups, stews, and tagines.

Black Pepper

Ground black pepper comes from the tiny, dried berries of a plant called Piper nigrum. It's best when freshly ground but it can also be stored a long time without losing too much flavor.

White Pepper

White pepper comes from the same plant as black pepper. For white pepper, only the inside of the berries are ground up. It's milder than its black counterpart. It's frequently used for the sweeter of the Moroccan sauces, especially those made with onions and threads of saffron.

Sweet Paprika

Paprika is made from ground-up red sweet peppers that have first been dried. It's used to season meat. It's also used in soups, stews, and bean dishes.

Cayenne Pepper
Also Called Hot Paprika

Like sweet paprika, this spice comes from ground peppers, although it uses a spicier type than sweet paprika.

Cumin

Cumin is created from the dried fruit of a type of plant in the parsley family. It is very pungent and gives a slightly bitter taste. It's used to spice eggs as well as stews and tagines. It gives extra flavor to meats that have been grilled or roasted as well.

Cinnamon

A sweet spice that is very fragrant, cinnamon comes from the ground-up bark of the cinnamon tree. Moroccans use ground cinnamon and they also use ground bark in the form of sticks or quills in their cooking. It's commonly found in pastries and desserts, but it's also found in entrees that combine meat and fruit. It's also used in harira, which is a traditional Moroccan soup.

Saffron Threads

Saffron threads are cultivated from the saffron crocus flower's stigmas, which are the sticky parts in the center of a flower. Only a few threads need to be used to give the dish a yellow color, distinctive taste, and wonderful smell. In Morocco, saffron is more affordable than it is in North America where it's more expensive to purchase.

Yellow Coloring

This orange powder is mostly used by itself or with turmeric to give entrees a yellow hue. By itself it has no smell and no taste. It's also quite messy to use!

Turmeric

Ground turmeric has an earthy smell and a somewhat bitter taste. The roots of the Curcuma Ionga plant are used to cultivate turmeric. It's frequently used with yellow coloring to give the dish a hue that looks like curry.

Anise

Both anise seeds and ground anise are used in Moroccan cooking. Anise has a licorice-like flavor, as does fennel seed, which is sometimes used as a substitute.

Nutmeg

Nutmeg comes from the seed of the same fruit that gives the spice called mace. It's both sweet and spicy, and is used in the traditional ras el hanout blend.

Sesame Seeds

The hulled white seeds that we think of as sesame seeds in the United States are not the same type of sesame seeds used in Morocco. Moroccans use gold-colored sesame seeds that are un-hulled. They taste nutty and are used mostly in baking and as a dish garnish.

Gum Arabia
ALSO CALLED GUM ACACIA

Arabic gum is ground and is used as a stabilizer. It comes from an acacia tree's sap.

Mediterranean Dry Rub

This mixture is used on grilled lamb, chicken, or beef to give it an exotic taste.

Fenugreek Seeds

Known as helba, these seeds have a gold color and strong smell. They are bitter if you chew them, but they give a sweet, unique flavor when cooked with an entrée. They are used in a small number of Moroccan dishes, mainly rfissa, a special feast dish made with chicken and lentils.

Bay Leaves

Whole bay leaves are cooked in stews, tomato sauces, and tagines. They are very aromatic and are sometimes taken out of the finished dish before it's served. They come from a certain type of evergreen tree.

Famous Moroccan Spice Blends

In addition to the spice blend called ras el hanout, Moroccan cooking has lots of other interesting spice blends. Here are some of the traditional blends used.

Moroccan Chicken Blend

This spice blend has a little sweetness coupled with earthiness and subtle heat. It's used in the tagine dishes made with chicken or other poultry.

Moroccan Vegetable Blend

A combination of spices including cumin, chili powder, coriander, sweet paprika, allspice, cayenne, clovers, allspice, and cinnamon gives a unique flavor to roasted or grilled vegetables.

Harissa

Made with chili peppers, olive oil, and paprika, this condiment is a paste that is spread over meat or bread. It's frequently used in couscous, which is a semolina in granules made from durum wheat that's been crushed.

Berbere

This spice blend includes many different spices with an emphasis on the heat from different types of peppers. The delicious flavors of Moroccan cuisine are served in restaurants all over the world.

Awesome! Now you know more about the aromatic spices and cuisine of Morocco. You can find more Geography and Cultures books from Baby Professor by searching the website of your favorite book retailer.

Visit

BABY PROFESSOR
EDUCATION KIDS

www.BabyProfessorBooks.com

to download Free Baby Professor eBooks
and view our catalog of new and exciting
Children's Books

Made in the USA
Monee, IL
22 July 2024

62358453R00040